The Mother's Tongue

HEID E. ERDRICH, author of *Fishing for Myth* poems from New Rivers Press and co-editor of *Sister Nations* anthology from the Minnesota Historical Society Press, has won awards from The Loft Literary Center, Minnesota State Arts Board, Wordcraft Circle of Native Writers, and the Archibald Bush Foundation. She founded Birchbark Books Press with her sister, author Louise Erdrich. Her degrees are from Dartmouth College and Johns Hopkins University. A member of the Turtle Mountain Band of Ojibway, she was raised in Wahpeton, North Dakota where her parents taught at the Bureau of Indian Affairs boarding school. She teaches at The University of St. Thomas.

Earthworks Series
Series Editor: Janet McAdams

To The Friends of the Library

The Mother's Tongue

HEID E. ERDRICH

Heid E. Erdrich
Hamline Branch
— 2006 —

SALT

CAMBRIDGE

PUBLISHED BY SALT PUBLISHING
PO Box 937, Great Wilbraham, Cambridge PDO CB1 5JX United Kingdom

© Heid E. Erdrich, 2005

The right of Heid E. Erdrich to be identified as the
author of this work has been asserted by her in accordance
with Section 77 of the Copyright, Designs and Patents Act 1988.

First published 2005

Printed and bound in the United Kingdom by Lightning Source

Typeset in Swift 9.5 / 13

ISBN 1 84471 060 2 paperback

SP

1 3 5 7 9 8 6 4 2

For John, Jules Ezra, and Eliza Jonis,
who taught me the mother's tongue.

Contents

Acknowledgments

Some of the poems in *The Mother's Tongue* were previously published, sometimes in an earlier form, in the following publications: "Idol Construction," *The Talking of Hands* anthology, New Rivers Press, 1998; "Stung," *Flyway* literary review, 2000; "Elemental Conception," *Borealis Literary Review*, 2002; "She Dances," *Sister Nations: Native Women Writers on Community*, Minnesota Historical Society Press, April 2002; "She Dances," and "Offering: The Child," *Cream City Review*, 2002; "Remedy," *Shenandoah*, 2004; "Image and After Image," *Great River Review*, 2005.

The author wishes to acknowledge with gratitude The Minnesota State Arts Board, the Archibald Bush Foundation, The Loft Literary Center, The Anderson Center for Interdisciplinary Arts and The University of St. Thomas for support during the period in which these poems were researched and written.

My sincere thanks to Chris Hamilton-Emery and Salt Publishing. Humble thanks to my mother, a.k.a Cyber-Kookum, for her beautiful artwork and her kind teaching. Many thanks for editorial comments to Leslie Miller, Janet McAdams, Roni Natov, Mark Turcotte, and especially Jim Cihlar.

Chi Miigwech to Rick Gresczyk, Gwayakogaabo. Nimiigwech-iwendam wiidookawiyan Awanigaabo. Miigwech Nimise. Miigwech Aanik. Miigwech niiji gikino'amaaganidok. Bungi etago ninitaa Ojibewem. Niminwendaan Ojibwemowin. My mistake's with Ojibwe language are mine alone.

Deepest thanks to my sisters and my neighbor-mothers whose humor pulled me through. Miigwech manidoog.

Offering: Words

Gichimookomaanimo: speaks American, speaks the Long Knives' language

Mother, if you look it up, is *source*,
(fount and fountainhead—origin,
provenance and provenience,
root) and *wellspring*.
Near her in the dictionary you will find
we all spring *mother-naked*,
(bare, stripped, unclothed, undressed, and raw)
with nothing but *mother-wit*
(brains, brain-power, sense) our *native wit*
with which we someday might *mother*,
(nurse, care for, serve, and wait on)
if we don't first look it up and discover
the fullness of its meaning.

Such interesting language, this *tongue*,
(our diction, idiom, speech, and vernacular)
also *sign language*,
(gesture language)
and *contact language*,
which was English or Ojibwe,
either way; both spoke forward our *mother country*,
our *motherland* (see also fatherland,
our home, our homeland, our land)
called *soil* in English our *mother tongue*,
our *native language* that is not my *Native language*
not the *mother language* Ojibwe:
wellspring of many tongues, nurse, origin, and source.

1 Honey Sweet

Craving Honey

Not the African bird, not the Honey Guide
who dives the honey badger,
or any human who comes near.
Not the bird who leads beasts
to the bee tree, then begs its share.

Not the bird calling "*Eat with me!*"
whose people, now forced from the bush,
ignore its cry in the rush of African suburbs.

No, not the bird, but the printed path,
the iris landing strip marked to show bees
right into the nectary, to drops
deep in throat-open flowers.

Not what we expected—that bees need a map.
Still our search for sweetness can go hard,
the signs often uncertain, the comb,
when we find it, locked in a wax tough to crack.

Not what we always thought,
that the blue flag unfurling meant to lure us,
when all along the iris wanted only bees.

Not the bird, not the flower.
No mystic hint of what it is we want.
Only a lane in print on furred petals.
Only the beeline. Only what points the way to.

The Way To

In the dimly lit cosmos of the body
one egg turns planet-like, its gravity
draws currents through a woman
like tide pull in caves by the sea.

Try to keep such images revolving
when even benevolent passion
seems too close, ironic, unnatural.

Not one of your girlfriends will ever
describe the actual moment:
How her eyes might have wavered,
tilted to his, her chin a perfect emblem,
sweet offering of someone wholly else,
and a bondage gone to willingly.

Certainly no one mentions
the little fear cries. Aloud or silent,
who knows for sure.
Some women hear both at once
Not me! And the twin call *Let me!*

The risk of stage fright's greater
the bigger the production.
Forget what it is you mean to do.
Make dinner, pay bills, wash the car.

The moment will come upon you.
He closes your eyes with kisses.
Aims his love and you pray he misses,
then you un-pray for days.

She Dances

The drum begins and she
raises her hand to lift
the female-feathered fan.
She moves slowly, heavy
in her buckskin, heavy
with the possibility of life.
Her neat fringe beats along
with the drum as she steps.
Full sun in full leather and
she wills herself not to sweat.
I pray the long days in the arena,
nights sleeping on the ground,
make her ready to dance labor.

Though it's my right, I never dance.
Not in a shawl, with fluid moving fringes,
not with beads offered up leggings,
no satin-worked ribbons or cones sewn
in V-shapes have ever drawn an arrow down
my hips to point the way to being woman.

But I once dreamed my friend a dress:
one in slipping honey colors of satin
with black bands. Its music came with,
its cones jangling and flashing near each
flower-print cloth outfit then on to the next.
And now I dream her another dress,
the one for labor, a traditional deep blue,
the midnight wool blue shot with red
that all her ancestors would recognize,
the heavy dress of history,
the one made of flags
and ration blankets and blood.

The Hive Improvisation
(dream in clarinet)

I hold out my arms,
take up the hive.
Their buzz shocks
through me alive
and I believe them.
In the blueness of a tank,
they come at me numb.
They say they are the drum
and I believe them.
The look on them is fever.
They shake me through forever.
The shy gut of me relents.
The hooks they shoot bend.
I hold out my hands, attend them.
The look of them is never-ending.
The things they say are blank
and I believe them.
The blue light they cast remains.
The look of them reminds me.
The sound of them surrounds me.
The things they say are true
and I believe them.
Their flowers flood my veins.
The hum of them remains.
They tell me I'm the same
and I believe them.

Weeds in Grief

There's a hound along the fenced lot
whose blue eye, whose green eye,
watch as I stoop, take a weed up
shake it by the root,
shake a victory over its insistence.

Plantain, White Man's Footsteps,
not native, an invasive—
no easy way to live, but to eke,
to creep in dry, packed earth,
where the hope of sun's enough.

Weeding in suicide's aftermath,
the hound dog bays at my wild laugh,
I stoop again, shake again
the tangled core of the thing.

Noxious. Alien. Stubborn.
I grub it out, yank and tumble back.
The dog whimpers as I gasp:
See how each root barbs to hook?
This life that holds so hard,
I have it all in my hands now.

Intimate Detail

Late summer, late afternoon, my work
interrupted by bees who claim my tea,
even my pen looks flower-good to them.
I warn a delivery man that my bees,
who all summer have been tame as cows,
now grow frantic, aggressive, difficult to shoo
from the house. I blame the second blooms
come out in hot colors, defiant vibrancy—
unexpected from cottage cosmos, nicotianna,
and bean vine. But those bees know, I'm told
by the interested delivery man, they have only
so many days to go. He sighs at sweetness untasted.

Still warm in the day, we inspect the bees.
This kind stranger knows them in intimate detail.
He can name the ones I think of as *shopping ladies*.
Their fur coats ruffed up, yellow packages tucked
beneath their wings, so weighted with their finds
they ascend in slow circles, sometimes drop, while
other bees whirl madly, dance the blossoms, ravish
broadly so the whole bed bends and bounces alive.

He asks if I have kids, I say not yet. He has five,
all boys. He calls the honeybees his girls although
he tells me they're *ungendered workers*
who never produce offspring. Some hour drops,
the bees shut off. In the long, cool slant of sun,
spent flowers fold into cups. He asks me if I've ever
seen a *Solitary Bee* where it sleeps. I say I've not.
The nearest bud's a long-throated peach hollyhock.
He cradles it in his palm, holds it up so I spy
the intimacy of the sleeping bee. Little life safe in a petal,
little girl, your few furious buzzings as you stir
stay with me all winter, remind me of my work undone.

The Way To Have No Child

Besides, who could face
all the daycare decisions,
like cracking yourself in half
my friends tell me.

Or when I think of those countries—
brown dust that gives up nothing.
How could I trade one life
for the look in the eyes of ten small girls?

In the morning, my love brings me coffee.
I write to you, to those girls, to the world.
No one screams in instant need.
There's toast and a magazine,
laundry on the stair.
These things will always be there.

A child grows wild, that's a risk we know.
Our whole herd of teenage nieces
and nephews wave their manes, whinny,
and gallop off when we come near.
Still, they flare their nostrils,
watch us from a distance.

We should have done it years ago,
dumb in love
when just a look could have split us
two into one thing.

Who knew? Who knew how long
we would take with each other?
There is a thing called the world
that just kept coming at us,
and at our door no unexpected guest
has ever been refused.

Stung

She couldn't help but sting my finger,
clinging a moment before I flung her
to the ground. Her gold is true, not the trick
evening light plays on my roses.
She curls into herself, stinger twitching
gilt wings folded. Her whole life just a few weeks,
and my pain subsided in a moment.
In the cold, she hardly had her wits to buzz.
No warning from either of us:
she sleeping in the richness of those petals,
then the hand, my hand, cupping the bloom
in devastating force, crushing the petals for the scent.
And she mortally threatened, wholly unaware
that I do this daily, alone with the gold last light,
in what seems to me an act of love.

The Way To Be Convinced

People will ask
why you have no child.
Say you don't know *how*.
You know the basics—that's not it.
But you wish for some ritual to convince you.
You've heard that rabbits dance,
elk sing deep, and just yesterday,
out your breakfast window,
two mating squirrels crouched
in the bare tree, one tail looped up,
one tail looped down,
making the sign for infinity.

In the dark, or in the early light,
some skipping kisses to close your lids,
some cooing song that rocks you past fear.
That's the way it should be done.

Or with some stunning certainty,
lovers should go down, invite lightning
to strike—their only touch to shade
each other's eyes when the blast comes.

This Body, The River

After a painting by Jim Denomie, Asiginak

Phthalo: All that time I ran underground, green as mud.
                           I didn't know I would flow until
                           some boy stretched out with me by the river—

Cadmium: stretched me to my water self,
                           my still but moving center
                           that entered me in the spring
                           still cool enough for breath to come
                           in clouds and me so young I thought it was love

Ultramarine: to be so close to the dark movement of water
                           in the hard bed, through frozen river banks
                           bristling with new grass and just that once

Titanium: just that first time, this body, the river
                           flows around stones, whorls an undertow,
                           makes a map, borders another territory
                           divides up the whole wide wet world.

Neon Lovers, Another Painting

Blue girl/hot pink girl
Pink boy/electric blue boy.

When they touch
little sparks
dance in their fingers,
gnomes in their bones
want sex.

Who are we to say no?
Too late, anyway—
The frothy lake rolls its tongue
the hummock hills cleave
the wind heaves deep sighs
the trees tangle limbs
shake their hair
and the very sun fires their skins
bright as after-sex angels.

For Her Sake

Water that fills a rock ledge,
sand that takes the shore.
She stands where we've all stood.

So it is when one we love comes to harm.
We wish that she brim, fill with calm,
but we know it's no good to turn her
from the future she strains toward.
We might as well unchain her.
She will step right off those rocks
and in that instant yawns the blackest sea.
Still we think, *Saving her saves me.*

She in a gown of fog with blue shawl trailing.
She gone so deeply into herself
that everyone goes right in after her.

No good the pocket of crusts,
No good the path of bread crumbs—
useless in such tossing waters.
No good those stories we grew up on.
Tell her another.
The lady's maid heaves a stone,
sets her mistress free.
Little girls lop giants off at the knees
or shout them to stone.
Stories to make grown men afraid.
Tell them new—for her sake.

The Red Toad

One morning in a girl's bed,
a red toad, a lump, hops
right into her lap.
She feels sorry for it—
helpless, bubbly, ugly,
yet hinting at transformation.
She's no fool,
she senses the mythic
at work in the vile.
She puts the creature to her breast.
In a while it smiles up at her—
Then she is caught, she feels a catch,
the red lump latched in her chest.
She knows what it is they won't tell us:
How we are born women without hearts,
born only the body
that will go on making other bodies
until blood and muscle
become spirit within it.
And so we too must trust transformation,
know it is our only story—
We are sea fissures that suffer change,
lava caves, vats to cast raw minerals in,
that cast up treasures in forms
smooth and glowing as red gold.

Oyster Mother

There once was a woman who worked
by the sea digging shellfish. Every day
she cried because she had no child.
Then one day a chip of oyster shell
flicked into her eye. Her teardrops
fell into the pink half-shell and formed
a shiny little boy with white hair.
She took him home, cradled him
in a bottle cap and you can bet
she never shed another tear.

Oh, what was it like?
The bivalve slit open alive, did it
believe it had produced a pearl?
Or the childgrain, the pearlgrain,
was it present in the wet eye?

Out of the world's irritation,
our wet insides should produce,
should pearl gritty girls who swim
in the oyster eyes of their mothers.

Amazon Huntress Gives Birth to Twins

Twin boys.
And then what is she to do?
With her single breast
and their four grasping lips
making wet O's of need—
She has to be clever, inventive.
They're only hers until weaned,
then banished as all men.
She wants all she can get
of the boys. But even she
almost gives up in the red face
of their famished cries.
And who could blame her?
There's no explaining to a babe
that it has to wait its turn.
Her bow arm's bulked mightily
so she holds her firstborn to her chin,
his bottle grasped in her mouth,
while the other son nurses wholly
sucking soul into body,
all the while gazing at the bottoms
of his brother's feet.
This is the memory she will send
with two sons cast into the world of men.

With Honey from the Rock Would I Satisfy You

She never wears prints with flowers.
A smart woman learns early
to salt the pit of herself, be serious,
and not bloom past her borders toward
unordered femininity.

Hot house roses barely brush
the hard center she prays into herself.
When nothing blooms in her any more,
she begins to think of the Bible.
What country was it . . .
the ground sewn with salt?

She can reach no tender part,
only callous and dull pain,
always the two,
nothing to rub her down,
no salt, no balm, but days
and those seem nothing to trust.

She thinks she might carry a child,
admit a new self into the hard case
of the old self, as in the Odes
when Solomon sang:
My heart was split and a flower appeared
and grace sprang up for my God.

She laughs in her bed
when she hears herself pray:
Honey, honey, come in me!
to man or God or child,
she does not know,
but surely it will take all three
to enter such amber sweetness—
honey in rock and twice as hard.

Woman's Work

All around us women are working
for babies like they're angling for promotion.

Over the gray flannel dividers,
through the hiss of secret business
they swap phrases that sound lovely:
Fan-shaped, trumpet flared, fallopian,
anomaly, resonance, ovum.

They plan and manage strategically,
We'll get the diagnosis.
We'll take a few days off.
We'll make another appointment.
No, I'd wait to tell the boss.

We know it's not our business,
but who could ignore
the music in the hiss:
Pelvic exam, tilted womb, another cyst,
read all the literature, kept a journal,
some new findings, full report.
We have another appointment.
No I haven't told the boss.
Six weeks for a delivery,
adoption gets two weeks off.

Pica

If she craves clay or chalk, or coal, she should be given cooked beans with sugar.

TORTULA

I

She drove the Honey-bun delivery van
well into her ninth month.
What she wanted she got hot off the rack:
coffee cakes, cake doughnuts, sweet rolls.
That cake, she says, brought my grandmother's
house right into my mouth. *Yellow, yellow*
as a kitchen in the fifties. Her eyes glaze.
No one could stop her from dunking for comfort
as she drove. Her tiny frame took the weight
in sweet elastic rolls. Dough, she sighs, egg dough—
that's what I made my girl of.

II

Water calls them down to the edge
to watch the wash and smell how
earth gives in, suffuses, makes them flare
at damp spring scent from underground.
Dry horses can follow their noses miles and miles
to what they need. It's that old instinct asserted
early in pregnancy: see them down by the lake,
women walking at the marshy margin of the bed,
hungry women with one appetite, women up early
to bend and touch mud to their tongues,
women out to eat the world.

The Deep

Sparrows up the column of the maple
make a god awful racket first thing,
first light, ever since April. The little twerps
are easy to read: I need, I need!

The adults, hysteric with lusty pride
simply shriek and shriek without message.
They wake the newly pregnant woman
who cannot at first identify her feeling,

but remembers another dawn, an outing
by sea to watch for whales. Who ever honestly
expects to see creatures so ancient, so huge?
Now she rides the same unexpected waves

of sickness in unstoppable rhythm, in swells
that tossed her hanging, wretched at the rail.
No one else saw the great humpback whale
who eyed her, alone there at the back of the boat.

The birds' persistent racket, the jets at take off,
sound to her ill brain like doom. She blocks it all,
hangs on her emblem of belief: the rolling water,
the great being revealed, real, watching her from the deep.

2 Salt Lick

Craving, First Month

My belly rejected everything but a certain sky,
the one that rocks the high north plains of home.
Nothing but color and light for my mouth,
streaks of cirrus like pale lettuce—tear a leaf
and taste that clear covering of clouds!
I craved the prairie. Wild as Rapunzel's mother,
I would have paid the witch's price,
but my dear sister agreed to drive
into the horizon, north and north for hours,
the car skimming along the two-lane blacktop
between acres of flooded field. We were asea
in the land that bred us. It fed us and we were happy.
The rush of passing color like fuel—
waves of chartreuse—mustard weed lapping the ditches.
confusing waves of sky grown on earth—flax blue as mirage.
Then a doe, then her blazing fawn springing ahead of us
red against the new crown of hard winter wheat.

That's what I grew my son on, month one.
I went hungry into the flat north
toward the reservation.
I ate it all.
Even the dusty green of the little-leaf sage
that covers my grandparents' grave
tasted good in my eyes.
Here it is, I said into wind up the bald hill.
Here it is, I said to the question mark of child.
Here's the land we are born from. Here's what made us.
Here's the world that fed us. Here now, you eat too.

Offering: The Child

We need a salt lick
to draw the deer-child,
the wild soul hovering
at the fringes of our existence.
We need to ask it home.

Or if we had a photo to post
like the ones we see at rest stops
that tell the world this one is wanted—
Come Home.

How to know what to offer,
what life it is that we offer?

We have nothing to lure
a whole new being
out of the tree edge of the future,
across the snow sweep of days
into the ring of our lives.

Finally we offer what our own fathers gave:
Names of ferns and birds,
the Purple Martin house posted each year
so now blue wings mean hope to us both.

We offer the wild rides with our mothers:
dented fenders, cars forgotten in the lot,
the Neapolitan melted on the dash.

In the end, we ask it as a favor:
Child, return us to days we thought were past.
Bring our grandmothers at the clothesline with you.
Bring our grandfathers in denim coveralls back.
We will all go berry-picking more often.
We'll do it right this time.

When I Go Down to Pray

The icebox breaks my fall,
graces me with cool tea, hot salsa
and white cartons of cottage cheese.
My grandmother had only one of these
in her larder. Hard we cannot go back there,
to her kitchen with its stiff aprons and haze.
She worked like a man to deserve her food.
Good pickles with butter, cheddar slabs
and better, best, her summer sausage
and boiled eggs and white rolls beside
every plate. You better sit, and don't forget:
you're gonna eat it all.

Kookum

Did she watch to morning? Tend the stove's fire,
her tiny infant boy nested in a shoe box, a crate
just his length that would do for a coffin, if she had to.

Was he like a boy from a story? So small he fit in a shoe,
slipped in with a wrapped and heated brick to incubate
this son who would be father of my own mother,

my grandfather whose Ojibwe words the wood's
edge heard daily and I heard too, rarely, mornings
when he bent, I now know, to offer pipe and prayer.

Did she fill the copper kettle? Kindle the fire
by her boy child, another of thirteen—the seventh,
and this one bound to lead his people, given Moses
as his second name—meant for politics and all of us.

Did she pray the rosary in vigil? Or call for Shyoosh,
her husband's sister who helped her deliver cures,
who delivered babies by the hundreds over many years.

Like sisters in a myth, did they sit up? Keep the child alive,
get him baptized, then take the buggy, ride to Canada
to ask for the same Indian Doctor, the Mashkiki Innni,
who later treated the mystery of great-grandmother's fits.

Did they manage it alone? Two women always proud to tell,
the story goes, how they warmed the tiny babies with a brick,
a box, and kept them breathing steam off of wet cloth.

We tell it now and you tell it later. Women will do as they must.
Or else none of us and less of them and not this story,
but the one with fewer questions and a far more certain end.

First Rice

for Jim Northrup

The grains should be green as river rocks,
long as hayseed, with the scent of duckweed
and sweetgrass that grows along the lake's banks.
First *manoomin*, feast plate laid for the spirits—
berries and tobacco offered with song.
What it must have meant to give
what little the people had to give:
herbs left in thanks for the food that will sustain us,
for the water that gives up that food,
for the world working the way it should
—living and full of living god.

Idol Construction

Take any one of the things you believe in:
spools, leaf-light, breasts, jars,
buds, shells, brown eyes, ponds,
glass marbles, a live firefly, the penis—
fill in the blanks and repeat:
I believe in <u>penis</u> as the soul of creation,
the <u>stiff</u> center of the <u>tower</u> of all
that makes us choose to live.
Oh <u>Penis</u>-eye-god defend me.
Then?
Then, the Everything-else-eye goddess,
raises you up, up, up
sucks you like ripe fruit off the rotten pit of self.

The Girl in Geography Class

The girl in geography class takes nice, legible notes
in capital letters, in pencil. The teacher ticks off facts
on another world she can't quite grasp though she
herself might have been FOUNDED thirteen years ago
by religious order and BORDERED by sisters on all sides.
The CAPITOL of her love? Fear.
She can map herself like a country she discovers.
In perfect blocks she quizzes:
LANDMARKS? Ancient forces left a chain of depressions
now known as Lazy Lake, Lake of the Shy, Care Less Lake.
EXPORT? The main export of her sex is shame.
INDUSTRY? Pressure treatment processes rage
into a soft, slow-burning fuel.
TRANSPORTATION? Any bike, any train, any boat, truck, or plane.

Advice

Settled in a great hump of green fresh grass
between wheel ruts in a field, you could get fucked.
Even if the grass is what you love, the boy only a way
to smell it all around you. The roadbed of warm sand
makes a soft couch. The grasshoppers, eyes starting,
will fling themselves away. The sun might begin to go down
in a stream of hot color. His cock could knock, knock
then press until he shakes. If you rear back,
you might somehow bring him in you.
Jets will etch milky trails across the blank blueness
above his hunching back. Get it over fast.
After that, give him nothing, not one touch of your green eyes.

The Bee Kept Wife

We laughed at his truck when he'd cruise up:
Eat My Honey each door urged
and on the tailgate a leering bee.
Something creepy about how
he kept hives by the river where kids
hung out drinking the near-beer he'd buy.
His teenage wife, we knew, had "a slow brain,"
and trouble carrying to term.
Sometimes we would see her in town,
ice eyes and poodle-perm hair.
Always some hitch in her walk,
filter-tip wafts over her shoulders like wings.
Didn't help she favored striped
and furry sweaters. She never flinched
when boys hollered, "I'll eat *your* honey!"
Maybe the smoke made her slow that way too, slow to anger.
She put up with the Bee Keeper a decade at least.
He slept out there with the bees, cases of 3.2 brew
and underage boys who each summer grew up and away.
And she's never looked one bit older, not at all.

Cat Woman

Just when she thought
she'd think a thought.
Damn, Damn, Damn.
She's got a top she's gotta blow.
Steamy ring and a volcano below.
Pity kitty her pleasure-less sex,
her painful getting on
with getting off. Just when
she thought she'd thought a thought.

Parade of Old Loves

Every night a different one returns:
his hair loopy curls or shorn
to velvet or in lanks or shiny bald,
he comes to me real as ever.
And I am utterly convinced each one
is the one who put this baby in me.
I take it as a retrospective show:
How things might have been—
This one's flat black eyes
on me again and me the same woman
I was once—as cold as he was hard.
I'm only waiting now to dream the one
I was all earth and warm for,
the one I lost with my belief.
I'll take this as my chance to retrieve
each part of me I loaned.
Come on guys, sure I'll say the baby's yours,
I'll make it bouncy, shining, golden just for you—
if only you bring it back, bring it all back,
so when I give this time, my gift is whole.

What Pregnant is Like

You get bigger.
I mean you enlarge,
diffuse, push boundaries,
cover the whole of woman,
man, and child. You balloon,
stretch in unexpected directions,
expand to contain whole lives with your
lone body. Your body becomes an extension,
a shelter built of love that takes the man in again
and again to hold all three inside. Such a good place,
such a good planet, so heavy you make your own gravity.

Young Poets with Roman Noses

The man beside me on the bench outside my college library
was the poet Milocz, but I did not yet know it,

as I admired his brambled eyebrows, his steady hand on the cup
while my own shook with nicotine and afternoon tea.

I was shy and unstudious, only out to glimpse young poets
with sharp features and perfect diction. There were a few,

and two of those would speak to me: One slight as a dancer,
the other muscled like a superhero sketch, all with lovely, lovely syntax.

I watched for them, came daily to free tea and did not know
Milocz sat beside me. When we spoke it was of the trees, the tea,

never poetry, bless him. That would have been beyond me.
I was expert only at love and thought I might love a poet-boy

if he would have me. I picked a bearded one from a distance whose nose
I described to my journal as roman, but not knowing what that meant

made my way past him to the OED. Oh, rich proximity!
He was there next to me. I forget what the dictionary told,

or what I might later have composed on the bench, although
twisting trees, red brick taken by ivy, lamps' rich pools on leatherette

were likely subjects in that time. I followed the poet boys to class,
found out the stature of my bench mate, never loved a one of them.

But how my fate clicked in those moments! Looking at noses,
wondering if they were roman, becoming poet by osmosis.

Years later a gentle listener came to hear me read and after
took my hand. His plan to marry a poet worked out better

than my own. And so I'd like to thank them, those young poets,
reach them—They led me to my life and love. Maybe they'll read

these lines and write, care of the editor. Maybe they will know
I'm grateful, I love my life. My life because of them, because of them
my love.

Wedding Blessing

Still, calm, a lake between them.

One says,
> *I see upon the surface of the water*
> *the unmoving clouds, the dark pines, the bones*
> *of birch and something more—*

The other says,
> *I see through the surface,*
> *through fog, through a wing of needles and cones,*
> *through the many-eyed whiteness of birch—*

The waters remain one sheer peacefulness.
> *I see you,* they both say in that clear moment.

Then the swirl washes between them.
And it is like that many times, many times—

Always one peering through for the other,
always the clarity in calmness and the waves after.

When one knows and says,
> *I have walked to the edge*
> *of myself, to my shore—I will always meet the lake.*

The other does not know but asks,
> *Am I the lake bed? The pebbles?*
> *This drift of sand and more?*

Together they say:
> *We have found the narrow edge, we have found the deep,*
> *we have learned to let these currents run between us.*

Then the pine with its dark green fan blesses them.
And the clouds in good rain, cool shade, shelter them.

The birch watching over them sighs and sighs,
makes music to celebrate this best wish, best wish—

They have made one thing of two.

Nesting Dolls

I've been golden in the long afterglow,
I've been that bubble in the honey pot,
I've been sweet, sweet in me
and all along someone else.
That's the mystery.
First the man gives up his driblet of will,
it leaves his body to enter mine and in a moment
start another body that will leave mine.
It's what we all crave and sense; the memory
of such harmony, then a series of losses, separations.
The egg, the gold bubble in me, once in my Ojibwe mother,
once in her Ojibwe mother, and so on back
like nesting dolls. Now we tip the jar,
watch the slow pour of gold, the bubble thins
grows toward self, toward that lovely love of self.

Craving, Seventh Month

She prepares a meal that's meant
to prove she's good for something
other than progenation, yet.

Vegetables cut with care, diagonals
of carrot quick to cook in cinnamon,
the dry rice in the hot pan expands
swells with currents and nuts.

She will place it all before her friend
who has come to talk of books, bitter
love, and politics—important things
and "No baby talk tonight."

Do the beeswax candles color it all?
Or is it, as she fears, her own glow—
that rich, that full? She pours sharp wine

to cut the monotony of tastes she now realizes
she's assembled on the plate: the maple glaze,
the sugared nuts, the fruit swaddled in cream.

There's no excuse she can find, though she tries,
murmuring, "Forgive me, it is all too sweet, too sweet."

Another Touch

We hold hands in a Minnesota movie house
in midwinter, the air a tropical fog of breath
left by matinee patrons before we sat down.
I turn my palm up in yours. An *oven* in my
last month, I would prefer the other picture:
cold murder done in manufactured snow
an hour north of here. But tension makes
the baby jump, so it's steamy Elizabethans
filling the screen with endless undressing.
The film's good, but my hand's as restless
as the hero's whose love is constantly undone
in hoops and laces and collars. My hand flips
over and over in the heat of yours, won't give up
this gesture, knowing how soon our touch
will be translated for the one we made of it.
The lovers on the screen are still undressing—
all those stays and jerkins and then, *good god,*
an excruciating unbinding. My hand rolls in yours
seeking to be warmed and cooled at once,
to be naked and covered at once. That touch
we've shared so long will soon give birth
to another kind of touch: kin to the passion
we've rocked out of our bodies all these years,
but played out in tender strokes to the one
who just now rolls across the walls of me to drub
its own small fists against what it cannot know as other,
what is still me, touched by you, not yet three.

3 Milk Sour

Offering: The Breasts

How does one learn *The Womanly Art*?
Shouldn't it be obvious how to use
our two most pointedly female parts?
Or at least natural as sexual arousal,
as inevitable and ballistic as orgasm.
Shouldn't milk just come?
Rather, there's a manual, not to mention bras
and accoutrements that look obscene
but turn out as utilitarian as churns for cream.

And so we will see, or not, if the books write
rightly, "Offer the breast," for all infant ailments.
Offer milk for cradle-cap, gas and tear ducts
sealed shut from cries that might last all night
unless you offer the breast, offer them work,
saying, "My Darlings, here's your use at last."

Craving Release

Evening primrose should egg the labor on.
Or it could make your body yawn and yawn
without real sleep for a week.

How can a whole person
grow at once so large
and stay as thin as tension
that holds water in a drop?
As curved as the edge of resistance,
bent to the point we break from self
into other selves.

This cannot happen, but it does.
Women blown full to shimmering,
inside attracted to outside,
whole, then parts, then parted.

We've been in bed forever with this lover
who has kept us on the brink of pleasure
until it's torture. Oh, let's just get it over.

Sisters Stay On the Other Side

Sisters there flows a river, dark green
or golden spring or a muddy channel
where we drown to the sound of lull-a-byes.

Sisters stay dry on the banks, do not even
touch toe to test the water. Stop your ears
when you hear siren sounds: wet, sweet wails
that insist you can never understand
life, love, woman, man—until you birth
or nurse or raise a child in this world.

Sisters stop your ears, ignore our voices,
garbled, gargled in the milk-stream:
You do not need these things to live,
though there is a life you will not live,
worlds wet with another atmosphere
you'll never breathe, yet still you breathe.

Sisters, stay on the other side, stay dry.
Someone must read in a pool of lamplight.
Someone must rise from the favorite chair.
Someone must leave books eased open.
Someone must hum to herself, pour wine,
hear only her own ear, un-tuned to our wet cries.

Image

My slicked up belly was the Ouija board.
The technician moved the wand over it,
clicked keys that stopped the flow of gray
and grainy shadows, images we couldn't read
but spoke to him in vague predictions.
The vital organs: click-click.
Length, rump to knee: click-whir-click.
The skull size, and *Look, this is hair* . . .

Then the face, the infant face, floated up,
seemed to peer at us, drifted like the moon
in clouds. After, we tried to picture it: heart-shaped,
bow mouth, deep eyes—but of course
what we had seen was only a shadow portrait,
just sound bouncing off the child's bones,
just echo, oh, oh, oh.

After Image

The midwife's scissors clicked just before the cut.
That sound alone was enough to make me drop
the baby in one push, but she yelled *Stop*.
I held his shoulders so they could lift the cord
noosed around his neck. They clamped it,
cut him free. And then the whole of him:
head-shoulders-hip-rump, those long, long legs
slipped through me. I felt him with my body,
saw him with my womb and open thighs.
Then they bundled the baby off to intensive care.

Close as a newborn, I held that early impression:
another shadow portrait in strokes my
naked body made, gray shapes in dim outline,
but oh, so intimately detailed.

After Birth

The placenta came, the pulsing afterbirth.
The midwife held it, tried to distract me
from the fact that my baby's lungs had collapsed.
I had brief interest in that mass, that bloody
constellation my son had gazed at all his life.
His side, his cosmos, pulsed still with bolts of blue
etched against the rich red that fed him.
My side bulged—a ropy mushroom of flesh, still shaped
like my waist and navel. "It looks like me,"
I said, and they all laughed. Then she lifted it,
gestured slightly in imitation of the presentation
of the child. I thought of the word *swoon*
and turned my attention to the wall.
That's how I missed the moment,
the actual second it was over,
pregnancy and giving birth
and the abstract notion of the child.

Postpartum I

Through the bright lens
of postpartum exhaustion
she sees herself go. The one she was
rips herself clear, slips quickly
into the quiet hospital bathroom.
She leaves with a zip, like cheap facial masks
you can lift away whole: nose holes
and eye holes—a shroud of skin.
That peeling sensation, that pleasant,
cleansing pain, that's how she tore away.
Nothing sheer about her as she walked off.
She went away raw, but completely fleshed.

The woman who remained, well,
she thinks, *That must have been me.*
Me before somebody new.
In mirrors and windows, the mystery
draws ridiculous inquiry:
Hello, how do you do?
How do you do and who?

Postpartum II

The baby cries. Though that describes
the truth of his cries as well as *crash*
describes the accident scene.
The baby goes off like a siren.
And the woman who stayed
wakes to comfort hourly, yes,
awake some part of every hour.
Forty-five minutes at the breast,
then the briefest rest, not the true slip
from consciousness but something like it,
like a hand in a pool skims its reflection.

Postpartum III

A child's needs are simple,
and confusing, and endless, and cruel
without our former selves to help us through.

But that self hangs back in the hospital bath.
All the time the baby cries, she sits on the tub edge
banging her heels, bored but no way she'd come home.

The shirker, the sullen, the teen-girl-child.
Nothing you pray brings her back
though every night you try to recall her,
pray she'll rush into the curled mother-form
that squeezes itself into a shell of sleep.

Postpartum IV

The woman who remained to be me smiled.
I could see her reflection waver
in the pools under the stroller's wheels.
She seemed happy enough.
Why not leave it at that?

Then someone,
maybe someone new,
began to form thoughts
Who are you now?
Who will be mother forever?

Postpartum V

You never know what a man can be
until he wakes along with you
in the boat of night.

He treated me so kindly,
as if I were someone he knew.

Remind me, I asked and he spoke
in a coaxing tone so girl I was
came near enough for me to see.

We three made our passage
safe through rocking waters
to the calms of our own dawn-fogged sea.

One day that girl worked her way
back into my laugh.
Welcome back honey,
I don't blame you—don't run off.

And our son opened the depths of his eyes,
so we both let go, let his huge blue soul
swallow us whole.

New Born

In the beginning
we had to say your name
to get you to stay.

Your body twisted in motions
practiced in the womb.
We tried to see the grace

you would have had in water.
Only your long hands swaying, gestured
something lovely. But oh, those constant

tortured jerks and spasms—as if you were not
quite in your body yet, but struggling in
as though into a too tight suit!

Even your eyes, your alien,
hematite eyes, when open in rare times,
seemed to belong to a creature only.

There was no human spark, just flickers, then dark.
We had to say and say your name, chant it,
call you into your body—

inhospitable though it seemed with its blood
bright in the skin, too hot or cold. Bouts of rage
left you shaking like a pup. And the hunger

that stabbed you every hour. Pitiful.
Why would you have wanted to stay,
if we hadn't said and said your name?

Where were you when we called?
A long echoing way off or near
as we sensed, tethered to the body

in an envelope so thin and shiny,
so hard and curved and reflective,
we could not see?

In the beginning we had to choose,
grab a line of words, find a name
that would call you from that place.

We said it and finally your eyes lit.
Your cord stump darkened and fell.
We sewed it into a pouch, a beaded turtle

whose legs point in the sacred four directions,
whose back holds up the world—this world
you now claim with your radiant, human gaze.

Look

When I say my son's eyes are like a lake
I mean they reflect that same slate blue
but with depth: rocky bottom, silt bottom,
currents shifting clear to night's deep lakebed.
I mean they *are* lake. Pure lake, no rusty metal,
barbed hooks, wrecks. Lake for all time.

When I say his eyes are like a lake
I mean lakes learned this look from him.

Breasts

One day I looked down
Imagine my shame
Bustin' out!
The blank buds
Have produced
Both nipples
Years later
The left more blind
My winking chest
Though boys groped,
Called me Chesty.
I never could grasp.
Some availability?

And there they were
Just twelve or eleven
Where were they before?
I wore so long could not
Such abundance.
Inverted, I heard
From my *male* midwife.
Than the bright-eyed right,
I hardly dared brush
Made horrible jokes
Why they fixed on me
Did my size advertise
I avoided sweaters for years.

Their true power,
I learned as I nursed.
Or even among friends,
Only you and the babe

Not to attract but to repel,
Whip them out in public
You will clear the room.
And the peace breasts make.

Twelve Items or Less, 1999

Anonymous woman on the cover,
at the checkout, in the national news:
Her breasts exposed as she marches,
cold, carrying a child whose need
grips me keenly in my own chest.
Why else the breasts?
Why the camera taking them, holding them to us?
Our eyes avert or invade, yet we suck—
Our whole nation nurses her now,
as she stumbles, numb, war-weary
somewhere out of Eastern Europe, safely away
from the moment she could return our gaze.

Popular Parenting
—in five poems—

Yet our entrenched modern belief that mothering maketh the baby persists
against all evidence to the contrary—bolstered largely by the expert advice
of childcare authors who, were they to discard the assumption that nurture
will necessarily triumph over nature, would find they had a lot less to
write about.
                                                — SUSAN MAUSHART, *The Mask of Motherhood*

POPULAR PARENTING: PEOPLE TO HATE AT 3 A.M.

Best-selling Dr. Ears.
And that simpering woman rocking
on the cover of *What to Expect* . . .
Your mother, every mother
you've ever met.
Dr. Ears,
some more.
Who was it rang the bell at nap?
Hate the postal carrier.
No, she is good.
She brings the world to your door.
She steps right up to the mouth of the volcano,
drops in offerings, small effigies:
bunnies that rattle at sacrifice
and wet-eyed ducklings
who give themselves up
with solemn, wheezing squeaks.

POPULAR PARENTING: QUESTIONS TO ASK AT 3 A.M.

Which is the volcano:
the baby's mouth, or the breast?

What makes men quest after God?

What woman who has birthed has not seen God?
The small, vengeful God
with the huge God voice.

What woman who has mothered has not known God?
God swaddled, hushed, fleeing the edict . . .

When can we go back to hating Dr. Ears?

.

POPULAR PARENTING: AGAIN, PEOPLE TO HATE AT 3 A.M.

Dr. Ears.
Good and hard this time.

And the singed outline of that simpering woman
who *once* rocked on the cover of *What to Expect* . . .

Your mother, every mother
you've ever met. *Prevaricators.*

And fathers too, for being a part of this,
for being able to stand apart from it.
Especially that eight -time dad,
Dr. Ears—
whose own lobes stick out
like a goblin goody-goody
as he sneers from his books
that suggest women should
wholly sink themselves,
douse themselves in the milk
of motherhood and light
the match or baby will
never become attached.

POPULAR PARENTING: WORRIES FOR 3 A.M.

Worry that your baby will never learn to latch,
will bulldoze a puppy farm at seventeen, because you read
instead of maintaining "the maternal gaze."

Worry that your child will recover memories
of alien abduction like the ones we've all heard:
gray-faced figures who loom over you in the night,
who bring you to bright lights
where they do something mysterious, studious,
to your unmentionable area, to area 51, the diaper area . . .

POPULAR PARENTING: LAST FEW PEOPLE TO HATE
AT 3 A.M.

Dog walkers. Where the hell are they?
Wind-up toy makers. Can't they invent auto-repeat?
Classical station DJs who decide now's the time to chat.
And though it's grown less satisfying, try to muster
some firm resentment for Dr. Sanctimonious Ears.

Try not to forget, though the baby's lids finally do float shut,
how Ears dubs mother and babe "the nursing couple."
You who have forgotten what it's like to be a couple,
or who never were one. And how generous of the doctor
to suggest that Dad could use some rest. Or that a baby
might be content on Pop's hairy, milk-ductless chest.

Try to maintain the vigor of your disdain for such
oppressive rhetoric, because it's the best you're gonna get
and a jolt of indignation just might warm you through to dawn.

4 Bitter Root

Offering: Ojibwe

Some leaf taps the classroom window.
I am wondering what's the Ojibwe word for poem,
while my teacher says, *There is a spirit
who helps the language live.
We should make offerings to that alive
spirit and ask for help.*
Then he gives the quiz.
I bomb it because the words leap live
from the page to the open window
where the spirit catches them, quizzes:
*Was it the one who was trying to write a poem?
Tell her to open the window and drift an offering down.*

Sometime before the end of this poem
I go outside, try to ask that spirit,
who's got its job cut out, for help.
I think: *I do not have the right, the right words.*
And back beside my window: *I only have my poems.*
Then words drift, offering in their own right their own life.

Craving: Bitter Root

What I know of home—
tanned bed of dry, tall grass,
hot scent in August sun,
sweet oils baked by days
long as the globe of sound
surrounding us from a million wings
creatures strum to the sun, the sun,
the low-hung northern sun.
What I know of home—
car hung up on a rock,
out of the bush three brothers
walk, help carry the car off.
We drive and drive, drink the road.
What I know of home—
tastes sometimes like medicine,
take it in and let it out,
bitter root, *wi'sugidji'bik*,
the Indian physic that should cure all.
What I know of home—
nothing, nothing words won't heal.

Twin Bugs

Creamy tan, pinstriped in maroon,
custom Volkswagens cut me off
in mid-joy ride. This must be a dream
because I hate the highway.
But speeding along toward the skyline,
the IDS and all the high-rises big as life,
bigger and more life-like, almost landscape,
now I love the road and am delighted,
when I should be enraged to see
two driver-less twin bugs cut in front
from either side. Two green vanity plates read:
Waabaabigan,
Wajiw gete.
The people's car, convertibles, deep red interiors
in cushy leather, write down my lane:
White clay,
Mountain of old times, or
Mountain of history.
Two mysteries I translate imperfectly,
twin Ojibwe words that now also mean
to wake laughing from a dream
that leaps language from the chest.

Vermillion Hands Petroglyph

Red ochre on rock, this kiss you blew
in pigment that outlines your hand.
Centuries waved by, gesture sealed
with the lasting bond the sturgeon
taught us—her leaping look,
the bend of her linked spine,
saurian, ancient, enduring.

Teach me back into time
Until I know there is no time.
My hand in yours for years and years.

Our Words Are Not Our Own

We never write alone, but by a grace,
a blue silk threads our words,
makes our work both ancestor and elder,
descended of one through the other,
bound by ties that tug through time.

My words are not my own.
My words are never mine alone.
I never write, but writing comes
ink blue or pale as the spirit of the stories
who spins out a voice, a call I answer.

Place tangles with their words,
repeats them in rock's colors.
The shapes of rivers print
what we find we tell in turn,
and all unknowing, call it our own.

We never write alone, but by a ghost:
a blue spirit tangles our words
makes our work sister and brother,
related through strings we tie and tug
to pull us through the years.

Language breathes like breeze, blows words
we hear or ignore or wish we could.
We are nets and words our catch.
Or are we caught in word-woven webs,
where we tremble strings to the unknown?

Our words are not our own.
We never write alone.

Poem for Our Ojibwe Names

Those stars shine words right
into the center of the dream.

Gego zegizi kane.
Gego zegizi kane.
Maaji'am
Maaji nii'm
Maaji gigidoon.

So it is when we have our names.

We will not fear.
We start to sing,
to dance, to speak.

When we did not know him
the stick man, the running man,
came jigging in our dreams.
Always in motion like a wooden toy,
he sang *"Bakenatay, Bakenatay"*
so deeply his voice was a root.

So too the woman wrapped in red wool,
whose laughter woke us, *"Chi Wabeno."*
She spoke the word for dreamers—
then teased in diminishment, *"Waban-ish."*
Still her meaning took us years to learn.

Gego zegizi kane.
Gego zegizi kane.
Maajii'am
Maajii nii'm
Maajii gigidoon.

So it is when we have our names:
We will not fear.
We start to sing,
to dance, to speak.

It is not what you imagine,
no matter what you imagine.
Stars shine stories.
Words come speaking into our dreams.

They All Dream the Lake, Again

Flat and quiet, it dreams itself
right up against the house.
Or bright as eyes and deeply cold,
it surrounds the road, the important path
that would take or bring a loved one back.
Why does the lake come close? What has it to say?
Darling look out, look away. The rocking,
slow watery signs must convey what we keep close,
contained in the mind's locks and dams.

The lake has come up to the house, benign,
bottomless and it is up to me to cross, to tell
my old love some urgent message from his son.
But what? And why tell it through acres of waves?
Why does the tide come to the girl metal gray and sharp?
If the lake must speak, give it music, not metaphor's thin air.
If what we feel must go liquid in the night,
make us grow back to our origins,
make us creatures fit to breathe in it.

In the Belly

Of my baby
I breathe rushing waters,
his element,
his blue air.
And I do not even miss the land
though sometimes we swim close enough
to see creatures very like me.
They sin and love it,
sin and forgive and go on.

In the belly of my baby
I am born and born and born
into the world a convert
whose old ways had a tang,
who wanted to walk in the dust,
tagging the powder-heeled mind.

In the belly of my baby
I have escaped the old suffering,
the self no longer dogs me, her teeth
dull as knitting needles against a silver blade
even now swinging to infant need.

In the belly of my baby
I grow another stroke, a hand
as clumsy as another set of toes.
My mouth learns to paint,
and pigment tastes the same
as ink—a bit more rich and rank.

In the belly of my baby
I am home not alone.
In the belly of my baby
I have not forgotten sin and the city,
the mission I fled, and the purge
still to come one day and spit me out.

Mother of Sorrows

The world at war looks
just like it did the day before.
Rain in red leaves, smoky clouds,
chalk marks on sidewalks
where my son pretends at words.
He barely has language, yet he's pledged to serve.

Mother Mary gave birth to a son
in a time of war. In the sky, a Stormy Petrel,
bird gray as clouds, met her boy's birth,
meant he might fish, not fight.
She wound her sadness around them
hushed the pulse of the world
so war could not touch the two as she drew
the curtain of her hair about them both.

Like the other Mary, Magdalene in her weeping,
my wet hair has flowed across my breast.
Mother's milk mixed with tears tastes
the same salty-sweet as blood to our sons.
A babe will suckle on, unaware
that everything the world tells his mother,
she drinks deeply so she cannot help but think:
I have fed my son on sorrow,
I have made him food for war.

I'm no Mary. I'm neither virgin nor whore.
Yet, we want to believe the patriotism of the virgin,
the selfless-ness of the whore, when either Mary
might have cried: See this male body? I made it
of my milk, my tears—I'll kill him myself before
you bring him home cold from war.

Summer of Infanticides

In the year of the murdering mothers,
one throws her twins off a bridge,
rips bare her breasts, jumps herself,
cries, "Freedom!" to the July Fourth crowd.
A man dives in, rescues one son.
The deranged mother's plucked from the river.
But what a half-life for the brother.
What myth is this he will he live?

In the hot months of murdering mothers,
another runs a tub, familiar duty of
night-gowned mothers in oil paintings,
kneeling over rosy babes. But her damaged child
fed through a tube, suffers each breath until this.
That mother smothers herself in a crowded room.
She taught college—worked like all of us.

Not mothers only, not only summer,
but later that October, a refugee man
takes his daughter's thighs in one hand,
dashes her against the nursery doorjamb.
He says it was a fall. Friends say,
"Their baby wouldn't take a bottle."
As if that explains anything,
when in fact that might explain it all.

Last Snow

Dumped wet and momentary on a dull ground
that's been clear but clearly sleeping, for days.
Last snow melts as it falls, piles up slush, runs in first light
making a music in the streets we wish we could keep.
Last snow. That's what we'll think for weeks to come.
Close sun sets up a glare that smarts like a good cry.
We could head north and north and never let this season go.
Stubborn beast, the body reads the past in the change of light,
knows the blow of grief in the time of trees' tight-fisted leaves.
Stubborn calendar of bone. Last snow. Now it must always be so.

Changeling

You grow to gold, your glow
too much honey. I look away or,
rarely, allow my eye to rest
a moment on your shinning, sweet form.
Next to you, I am
so humble, such a bear,
all shag and fat and weariness.
Your mother is a bear who grew
to believe your loveliness must be
the work of tricky spirits.
Nothing else can explain the way
you hold her in your power.
Little son,
I will ask you now
because you are so easy in giving:
Forgive your mother. All her life
she has batted down the tree of bees
and barely felt the stings. Forgive her now.
What mistakes she will,
she will.

Elemental Conception

She wants to grow from the rich-rotten trunk
of the stump left to sprout in the chain-linked
alley yard. She wants to be born there.

Or out of dry wind rushing debris around
and cleaning the world like a slate that
hasn't yet written how her birth will be

if she be born slick-wet and shimmering
in rings like gas spill, born from long trickles
run off curb-piled snow that flows in curtains

any northern winter when it is possible to burn
in water, when flakes against skin so cold brand
their pattern on the new-thought, engraved self.

Maternal Desire

My skin means nothing without love's brush.
It goes full numb alone. Goes blank and dumb
untouched by nectar-thick flesh against my breast,
the sticky cheek's slight sting and the pulling away.

That's the taste on the mother's tongue,
the terrible hunger that licks out,
spreads like an aura—another skin.
Who will touch me? How can I stand this craving?
Another moment untasted, untouched, unread.

My husband's nubby head next to mine
and our breathe, into him, out of me. We. We.
These tense little bodies that wrestle me.
My boy, so fast I chug after for a snatch of him,
just to savor the body blow he hurls.
He never let me hold him, but on my lips.
No pictures of him but in motion.

Not one loved one, but in motion,
all headed out of my body, less needy
than needed, essential food, the have to have
that feeds my skin, that keeps my body, keeps me in.

1 A.M. Turtle Pool

Deluge in June, the lawn sodden,
the turtle's pond wells above her rock.
She arches her powerful striped neck,
claws meaning at the cement at my foot.
Then I do it—fit my hands to her back,
lift her slightly. She does not fight me.
Her notched shell faintly scrapes my palms.
Whatever she wanted, rescue's not it.
I let her down and she dives, circles, rises.
The dark water hides all but her ivory stripes,
her white smile that delighted my child,
who pounded the ground, cried
"Turto, Oh, Turto, Turto!" made the sign:
thumb arched under one cupped palm.

Floods once covered the world and a girl
held onto the same mud-green creature
long enough to be sure earth could hold there.
Safe and dry on her strong back, the little
turtles sun at noon in a stack. This is not
maternal gesture, just a way to fool birds of prey.
Threats and rain both come abundant from above.
Last night, I thought she'd be drowned and needed land.
But she's fine, better without us. She gets along.
Still, I feel the notches of her shell, her power
real and willful and scribed like words in my hands.

Remedy

Along the sloughs, the muskeg—
the pharmacy to the Ojibwe,
she gathered highbush fruit, pembina
for Lydia Pinkham's elixir.

They say Kookum could cure cancer,
but her remedy no one remembers.
My grandfather helped pick the cranberries,
toted sacks to the train to weigh and trade.
He learned the herbs, now disappeared
as farms plowed the wetlands down.

Do you recall this grandmother?
Powdery sweet berries in snow—
She dug wild roots, took leaves.

Did she leave asema, the snuff she carried?
Or Aunt Shyoosh's kinickinick?
Stripped from red willow twigs.

Her cabin swung with bundled babes,
suspended in blanket cradles from the beams
where she dried her medicines:

Prairie Sage for hemorrhage,
taproots shaped like a man's legs,
swamp tea and slippery elm,
recipes knotted into the strings
that held the stems and the twigs.

They say she could cure cancer,
that her remedy died with her.
But plants tell their own power.
She could listen. Who will hear now?

Wiisah kote: The Burnt Wood People

They roll from the flames shedding,
emerge clean as wood leapt from its bark
and handsomely smooth as carvings.

This explains their knobby knees,
their knotty eyes and long-limbed ladies.
This explains their buried hearts,
their whispers in winter, their warmth.

We oaks, we old *mitigozhiig*,
rattle another season's last leaves,
hang them red against the north wind,
hold them as long as we can—
the last-leaved shelter on this savannah.

One hundred years ago, one hundred years from now,
we would stand over them, stand hard.
Let them remember their need for fire.
Fire that breaks the shell, that engenders the seed.
Fire that makes them, makes them over.

Wiisah kote: or Burnt Wood is the Ojibwe name for Metis.

Mindimoyeg: Dandelions
for Lincoln

I thought, why cut them out?
A weed so cheery on the boulevard,
first thing to bloom in Spring—
But the retired Emperor of the Neighborhood,
crossed the street, shoved a dandelion fork
in my hand, asked did I know what it was,
demanded I use it.

Who can blame him?
His whole generation groomed lawns
next-to-godly clean. Chemicals
and edger rentals: The American Dream.
My weeds might invade, take each lawn,
year by year until all this Spring cheer would
nod up and down the avenue.

That would not do. Not a fair fight,
since this species long ago arrived, took over,
became so valued by the people here
that they named it for their elders.
Mindimoya, Old Woman, Ojibwe call them.
White-headed in a day, yet full of seedy
vigor—most fertile once they've aged.

When young, the mindimoya helps
new mothers get their milk: notched leaves bleed
white sap, a bitter tonic that perhaps works
as a suggestive cure. Or is there science here?
So many of the old medicines have come to signify.

I might have tried it, had I been desperate to get
a baby on my breast. Nothing could taste worse
than hungry infant cries. But no, my son slept sated
in a basket nearby where I dug the milky roots,
all the while apologizing to the strong old ones,
asking that they give up their hold on the place.

And though I piled them high, blistered my hand
where the fork fit, next year they returned.
Our young neighbors made a pact to just let them go.
And the old ladies nod now, Empresses of the Avenue.

Old Man's Tale

A stump of a fellow, bumpy, brown,
low to the ground—called himself
Little King of Everything.

One day he spies a maiden,
Now she's a prize, he thinks.
Yellow-haired, arms notched and strong—
so lovely he looks away, thinking
I'll come another day to pay court!

Next time he hops by she has sisters.
Dozens of sisters, all shining-headed
with milky throats, all dancing to the sun.

How could he choose? *I'll have my pick,*
he thinks, and bides his time, spies all day,
sees the best, most beautiful, most fair.
In the morning, we'll wed! he swears.

By the glitter of the dew, by the yawn
of dawn, he comes hopping along.
Old ladies greet him, nodding heads
puffed with shining white hair.
They lean together singing:
Love waits for no one.
No one waits for love.
And so it is with everything,
Little King, Little King.

Basswood

Green and more green each night,
unfolding leaves, hand-sized hearts
that cleave to bright sprays.
Their scent hums across the darkness.
Honey drift brushes against us,
wets our mouths.
We speak like bees,
throats full of silky sweet:
Ozhaawashkwaabiigizi,
nininj, inde'.

Green and more green,
the Basswood groans
arms grown full with hand-waving hearts.

Ojibwe phrases: leaf-green, my hand, my heart.

Husbandry
for JEB

—my old dame will be undone now for
one to do her husbandry and her drudgery

KING HENRY IV, PART II: III, II

Funny how meaning changes,
escapes the farm for a lover's arms.
Chattel once *husbanded* take the loss,
live now simply as cows.
When did this dear word
stop its work as verb?
True, I am no man's crop,
but surely my darling practices
a certain agronomy on me.
Alternately, his household care,
his drudgery and parsimony,
his production of such domestic
creatures as wife and child
might define his kind of husbandry.
Truth, I could do with a bit
of the scientific management
meant by such a title. Husband,
husband me as a garden,
cultivate, till and raise me
to your level—
for this old dame's undone
without her beloved one.

The Good Woman
For Allison and Lise

The Good Woman's home makes up into beds:
pullouts that creak and plaid sofa-sleepers.
Piles of mongrel boys toss in every room,
strays with no where else to rest. She takes
them in, gives them each other, makes enough.

The Good Woman's screens all hang open,
or stand propped to beckon like a waved hand.
Her doors all stay unlatched, except one: behind it,
a high floral bed, or one plumped with geometrics,
and a broad or flat back she can curl her hips to,
or lock out, or leave alone.

The Good Woman's house or trailer or apartment
smells of the crockpot simmering bone and broth
and beans. It smells of foods that stretch to mouths
opening wider and wider each year.

The Good Woman wraps in wool and sits up before sun
on her porch or stoop or fire escape.
She smokes or takes tea hot or with a shot.
Across her lawn, across the street, down the sidewalk,
a path runs toward rail yard, bus station, truck stop:
all ways the boys leave, or find their way to her home.

The Good Woman holds out her hands to the blue dawn.
Beasts with heavy heads and twisting horns
bow down, breathe her in and sigh.
She has never known if this is a dream,
so she goes on waiting in the cold
for visitation, vision, benediction.

The Good Woman falls from another world, clutches
at roots and rocks and creatures as she tumbles.
Her hair rains over her face. She does not know time.
When she lands, in her pockets, in her hands,
all medicines, minerals, meat we will need,
all that the people must know to survive.

The Only Child

Would get a bath every night,
and songs and clean pajamas
printed with catalog-happy robots.

The only child would survive
fleeing beasts, pestilence, war—
safely held by two parents who know

you shouldn't have more children than
you can pick up and carry at a run—
better yet have one and share the burden.

The only child would wonder,
certainly, what others like him
might be. But his wonder would be luxury

uninterrupted by his sibling's cries.
Just a pause between whirlings of marvelous
mechanical toys—all his own.

The only child would glow
with the fine shine of stone
tumbled between us both.

And so, he gets a sister. She gets him.

Motherhood as First Language

The mother's tongue speaks to the realm we are returned to with our pregnancy and giving birth. Returned as transported visitor, gone through the portal, reborn as we birth there, made changeling — all of these, but not always that mystical journey: sometimes we return as kidnapped, hostage in a world of children. The mother's tongue is the language of that realm: our voice as both rule and guide, heeded and unheeded, some sound we ourselves can hardly hear and often voice beyond sound: gestures and sensations, the things at the tip of our tongues we cannot say.

The mother's tongue is language of the female body. We laugh, my friends and I who have become "old mothers" in our late 30's and even 40's. Nursing babies, we bookish women, we near spinsters, laugh because we could not have known, living so long in our heads, how powerful our bodies could be, once they had made other bodies. Why resist? I finally decided, why not admit and praise the desire we have for our newborns, our craving for sweet baby flesh in caress and even the odd attraction to their sourness—to all our hungers for their bodies that must be a part of their hunger for ours.

The mother's tongue points to the truth about those first months with an infant—nearly impossible to convey. To mother is to teach language, a great joy and saving realization that makes the tedium and exhaustion of early motherhood something we survive and from which we grow.

The mother's tongue speaks of postpartum as place between life and death—postpartum as haunting. We new mothers wander about in the wee hours in our gowns, ghostly, in the halls at all hours and haunted by our former lives.

The mother's tongue speaks our transformation in giving birth, of the ways in which we are transported or taken to a world we cannot always be willing to inhabit. And at other times we are the almighty ruler of a tiny realm that is infancy or childhood. The mother's tongue is the language of that realm: our voice, the things at the tip of our tongues we must not say.

My own mother's tongue, spoke encouragement, discouragement and courage. The mother's tongue of my poems is that as well, and it speaks to advice, the tyranny of advice to new mothers that somehow is never what we *wish* we had known. So the mother's tongue is the desire for the voice of mother when we are most vulnerable with our young children.

The mother's tongue is a recovered language that speaks how deeply in childhood we are with children. Reading to them, I re-examine the literature of childhood and let its language into my own poems and stories. What and how and when I read to my children gets to the roots of literature, of language, of story as it comes within the ultimate oral tradition—the same font that springs all stories in all tongues everywhere: The mother's tongue.

The mother's tongue is the language of the people, the speech in indigenous words that prays out of this land, into this air and that has from the earliest times.

And again, the mother's tongue is the Ojibwe language that my mother was discouraged from learning, that her father used in prayer, that was banned, punished, obliterated by government plan, and the power of the church, and by the sheer weight of trade language as survival language.

The mother's tongue is agile, adaptable, two-hearted or more. It defies the notion of adaptation as merely response to colonization. Adaptation is cultural survival and has always been so. I adapt my forms to speak across boundaries at once unreal and totally natural. Crossing-genre in the Ojibwe tradition is resistance and persistence and the breaking of an imposed silence. The mother's tongue is agile, it adapts and more. As response to an environmental colonization, it speaks in images of the invasive, non-native, yet comfortingly familiar plants and creatures we see every day.

The mother's tongue is ultimately the first story told from the first speech and maybe even before that in sign and song and symbol and tracings on clay and beads strung in reminder of story or song. It is that which resists all definition, that thing before, behind, beneath all telling. The mother's tongue is the language of earth, the words in rocks, and seasons as song, and all that speaks to me without human language—all that I have relied on for so long, that I pray will survive for my own children to praise and to know.

Notes

The cover artist is my mother, Rita Gourneau Erdrich. The 1994 mixed-media painting is from a 1912 postcard titled "Chippewa Mother and Child," of my great-grandmother Eliza McCloud Gourneau (Kookum) with her daughter Flora. The beads my mother incorporated into the watercolor replicate one of the few remaining pieces of my great-grandmother's beadwork. A berry peddler, an herbalist and a birth attendant, she also sold her beadwork to travelers to suplement income for her family of thirteen children. Embrodiered detail on the painting also suggests Kookum's skill in quilting which she did with clothing scraps and strings from tobacco bags.

1 HONEY SWEET

Pica. Pica is a form of geophagy, often occurring in pregnancy when women have irresistible cravings for clay, chalk, charcoal, sand and other earthy substances. The word pica is thought to come from the Latin word for magpie, a bird who eats odd things. The quote from Tortula and many other interesting facts can be found on *Medieval Women's Guides to Food in Pregnancy* by Melitta Weiss Amer http://www.cbmh.ca/archive/00000267/01/cbmhbchm_v10n1weissamer.pdf

This Body, The River inspired by a painting by my friend, Ojibwe painter Jim Denomie, Asiginak. The actual painting is viewable at http://www.maicnet.org/2rivers/nitelife.gif

2 SALT LICK

Kookum is Michif/Metis, from the Ojibwe word Nookomis, meaning grandmother. This is what my mother called her grandmother and how she referred to her when she told stories.

3 MILK SOUR

Twelve Items or Less, 1999 refers to the cover of the April 12, 1999 edition of *Time Magazine*, a special report on Kosovo titled "Are Ground Troops the Answer?" The cover is a photo of a refugee mother nursing her child.

Popular Parenting I–V refers to several texts, but especially sends up a revered baby guide advocating "attachment parenting" by a Dr. whose name rhymes with ears. A particularly oppressive book, it is none-the-less beloved by American mothers. Another cultural reference in this poem series regards a supposedly secret U.S. military installation where alien remains are kept called *Area 51*. My younger sister, a pediatrician, suggested we should give this nickname to our child's "diaper area" as doctors euphemistically call it.

4 BITTER ROOT

Ojibwe words are either translated below the poem or understood in context. Some words are the product of dreams and intentionally not translated or translated imperfectly so as not to offend the spirit of Ojibwe language.

Summer of Infanticides refers to actual murders that took place in 2002 in Minnesota.

Remedy mentions Lydia Pinkham's elixir, an American patent remedy for "female problems."

Mindimoyeg: **Dandelions** uses one of the Ojibwe names for dandelions that means *old women*. Another name, *dodo-jibik* refers to milk.

Old Man's Tale is adapted from a story by Wabeno Opiche.

Printed in the United States
43850LVS00003B/35